The Laws of Nature

Excerpts from the Writings of Ralph Waldo Emerson

Vicki and Sharon,

Happy Anniversary!!!

Love,

Tim, Patti, Tim Jr.

The Laws of Nature

Excerpts from the Writings of Ralph Waldo Emerson

Edited by Walt McLaughlin

Expanded Edition
with a New Introduction

HERON DANCE

HERON DANCE PRESS & ART STUDIO

Hummingbird Lane
179 Rotax Road
N. Ferrisburg, VT 05473
888-304-3766
www.herondance.org

Printed in China by P. Chan & Edward, Inc.

Heron Dance donates art to dozens of grassroots wilderness protection groups each
year. In addition, *Heron Dance* supports the Northeast Wilderness Trust with financial
donations. For more information, please contact our office at 888-304-3766.

Hardcover
ISBN-10: 1-933937-20-3
ISBN-13: 978-1-933937-20-5

Paperback
ISBN-10: 1-933937-14-9
ISBN-13: 978-1-933937-14-4

Cover art and watercolors by Roderick MacIver of *Heron Dance.*
Designed by Terry Fallon. Cover design by Luana Life.

For information about special discounts for bulk purchases for resale,
please contact Ingram Publisher Services at 800-961-7698.

Emerson has special talents unequalled. The divine in man has had no more easy, methodically distinct expression.

—Henry David Thoreau

Contents

Introduction

Ralph Waldo Emerson was the first American thinker to acknowledge the self-evident realities of the physical world, thus giving rise to a philosophy deeply rooted in nature. Thoreau came later, as did George Perkins Marsh, John Muir, and John Burroughs. In his slender volume, *Nature*, Emerson presented ideas that altered humankind's perception of the wild. The impact of those ideas is still being felt today, yet most people are not aware of that book or Emerson's heavy, naturalistic bent. Most see Emerson as a quaint poet, lecturer, and essayist of yesteryear and nothing more.

The Scottish writer Thomas Carlyle once said that the prophet and the poet are much the same. Both explore what he called "the sacred mystery of the Universe." No doubt Emerson stumbled across this notion in his youth when he first read Carlyle. No doubt Emerson aspired to be that kind of poet, seizing upon the laws at work in the universe, then conveying them to others.

Emerson took an interest in writing early in life, but those around him thought he should follow in his father's footsteps. Emerson's devout mother, as well as his Aunt Mary, urged him to become a minister. So that's what he did. Emerson studied divinity at Harvard College. In 1829, he became pastor of The Second Church of Boston. He married the young, beautiful Ellen Tucker a few months later, and lived for two years what appeared to be a perfectly normal life. Then Ellen died of tuberculosis. That tragic event sparked a spiritual crisis in Emerson. An ember that had been smoldering within him since his college days suddenly burst into flame. And before another year passed, Emerson was rethinking his vocation, his beliefs, everything.

During a sermon that he gave in the spring of 1832, Emerson issued a shocking statement to his congregation: "I regard it as the irresistible effect of the Copernican astronomy to have made the theological scheme of redemption absolutely incredible." Having said that, there was no turning back. Emerson retreated into the White Mountains of New Hampshire that summer to collect his thoughts. When he returned to Boston, he resigned his ministry.

On Christmas day, Emerson boarded a ship sailing to Europe. The following spring, he had an epiphany while wandering about a botanical garden in Paris. In the Jardin des Plantes, the natural order of things impressed him deeply. Emerson was astounded by the mysteries and complexities of the physical world. Shortly thereafter, he wrote in his journal: "I will be a naturalist."

In 1834, Emerson began lecturing in earnest. In 1835, he married his second wife, Lydia Jackson, who was more his intellectual peer than Ellen. They moved into a house in Concord, Massachusetts. There he worked diligently on *Nature*, which would be published a year later, in September 1836. And thus his true life's work commenced.

Emerson always enjoyed a walk through field and forest for its own sake, yet there is no mistaking the great weight that he gave the word "nature" whenever he used it in his writing. More often than not, that word was loaded with metaphysical significance. Hence the importance of his first book, *Nature*. In less than a hundred pages, he outlined a philosophy that recognized the hand of God in the world — the inexorable laws of nature. It was a new beginning for the renegade cleric. As Robert D. Richardson Jr. wrote in *The Cambridge Companion to Ralph Waldo Emerson*, "Nature was Emerson's starting point for a new theology."

In the introduction to *Nature*, Emerson wrote: "Philosophically considered, the universe is composed of Nature and the Soul." But what seems at first like a reiteration of the same old mind-body dualism actually runs much deeper. Spirit and nature are inexorably entwined in Emerson's worldview. You can't have one without the other. Hence, the *transcendental* aspect of his philosophy. The physical world that we experience firsthand is emblematic, pointing the way to a higher reality.

The Transcendental Club came into existence the same month that *Nature* was published. Its members often met at Emerson's house. Bronson Alcott, Margaret Fuller, George Ripley, and many other New England intellectuals attended those meetings, as did a handful of college students like Henry David Thoreau. The Transcendentalists embraced the writings of Goethe, Kant, and the German Idealists in general, but Emerson and a few others flirted with Eastern religions, as well. They were open to all sorts of possibilities.

Transcendentalism opened the door to brand new interpretations of nature. As Roderick Nash observed his book, *Wilderness and the American Mind*, the movement "gave forceful expression to older ideas about the presence of divinity in the natural world." Unfortunately, not everyone liked those ideas. When Emerson presented this new theology to the public in his "Divinity School Address," he encountered stiff resistance. Some people considered Emerson's naturalistic worldview quite refreshing. But others thought it was heresy.

The conservative clerics at Harvard were particularly displeased with Emerson. In *The Flowering of New England 1815–1865*, Van Wyck Brooks reports: "The Cambridge theologians reviled him: he was a pantheist and a German mystic, and his style was a kind of neo-Platonic moonshine." Emerson feared that the controversy swirling about his rather unconventional views would ruin his lecturing career. Oddly enough, it didn't. Most people attending his lectures were willing to overlook his religious idiosyncrasies. They marveled at Emerson's eloquence and profound insights, largely ignoring his pantheistic tendencies. Consequently, his lecture halls remained full.

In August 1837, the day after graduation ceremonies at Harvard, Emerson gave his most famous address: "The American Scholar." In that address, he challenged the younger generation to think freely, to root their thoughts in everyday life, and be truly American. "We have listened too long to the courtly muses of Europe," Emerson said, and many people in the audience, such as Henry David Thoreau, took this to heart. A half century later, Oliver Wendell Holmes would call that lecture "our intellectual Declaration of Independence." If nothing else, it marked Emerson's own liberation as a writer and thinker.

A couple months after the address, Emerson asked Thoreau: "Do you keep a journal?" and the younger man of Concord promptly began one. It is hard to say how much Emerson influenced Thoreau, but there's no denying that the elder man of Concord had some impact upon the younger one. We know, for example, that Thoreau read Emerson's *Nature* twice in 1837 — first in April, then again in June — and that the two men spent a great deal of time together during the late 1830s. Quite often they would go for long walks together. Both men mention these walks in their journals.

Because of the fourteen-year age difference between Emerson and Thoreau, we are tempted to call their bond a mentor/student relationship and leave it at that, but this denies the mutuality of their intellectual exchange. Thoreau was no mere imitator. Even a cursory reading of Emerson's journals shows Thoreau's influence. To some extent, it was a two-way street.

A careful reading of both men's works reveals significant differences, not only in style but also in content. While Emerson declares the interconnectivity of all things, both natural and social, Thoreau emphasizes individual action. While Emerson's reading was as eclectic as the subjects of his essays and lectures, Thoreau stuck mostly to the classics and gradually narrowed his focus to natural history. All the same, they shared a deep reverence for the wild. The words and phrases they used to describe various aspects of nature often mirrored each other. It isn't hard to imagine the intellectual cross-pollination that must have occurred whenever they got together.

In 1845, Emerson gave Thoreau permission to build a cabin on his land at Walden Pond. It could have been Emerson's axe that Thoreau borrowed to cut the trees for the cabin. In some way, Thoreau became the naturalist that Emerson had resolved to be back in Paris in 1833. The complexities of Emerson's life — his role as father, husband, lecturer, man of letters, mentor, and social leader — prevented him from being simply a thinker immersed in the wild, as Thoreau was for a while. Yet nature remained the driving force behind Emerson's worldview all the same.

The 1840s were a busy time for Emerson. Along with Margaret Fuller, he edited a journal called *The Dial*, which became a major outlet for the Transcendentalists. Emerson's book, *Essays*, was published in 1841, followed a few years later by *Essays, Second Series*. By 1845, his lecturing had taken off. He became famous throughout the country as one of America's freshest and most powerful voices. In 1847, he even published a collection of poetry. By the end of the decade, Emerson was a significant force in the literary world, both at home and abroad.

Despite Emerson's growing fame as a writer and lecturer, and increased travels as a consequence, nature remained the focal point of his worldview. He continued using the word "nature" to signify the organizing force in the universe. The natural world was more to Emerson than just wild animals, pretty flowers, and sublime landscapes. In fact, he discarded the original title of his first essay collection, "Forest Essays," as the work took on greater depth and breadth. He realized that the philosophical weight of his essays — what many consider his most potent work — was better served by rather vague titles. Above all else, Emerson wanted his readers to look beyond the romantic notions of nature so popular at the time and see the big picture.

In 1850, Margaret Fuller died in a shipwreck. This sudden and tragic loss of a friend came as something of a shock to Emerson. His worldview darkened somewhat as a consequence. He had already lost his father at an early age, his first wife, two of his brothers, and his five-year-old son, Waldo. During the 1850s, he would lose his mother and another brother, as well. Clearly death was a part of life, and nature was rather heartless and arbitrary about it. This notion first emerged in Emerson's journals, then appeared in his last great work, *The Conduct of Life*.

Initially given as a series of lectures, *The Conduct of Life* developed over time into a book. When it was published in 1860, Emerson was at the summit of his intellectual powers. In this book, he wrestles with some tough philosophical issues: power, belief, illusion, and fate. Here, too, Emerson reaffirms the wonder and beauty of nature without trivializing it. Natural science looms large in

The Laws of Nature

this mature writing. In his definitive biography, *Emerson: The Mind on Fire*, Robert D. Richardson Jr. wrote: "The more strongly Emerson felt the cause for tragedy, for waste, for chance, for loss, the more he looked to science as well as his own convictions for proof of underlying order."

Beyond *The Conduct of Life*, Emerson would live and work another two decades, but his best work was behind him. All the same, Emerson never lost his love of the wild. Even in his old age, he would go for a walk in the woods and marvel at the persistent mysteries of the natural world. No doubt he remembered walks with the nature-loving Thoreau in previous years. How strange that Nature would take Thoreau in midlife, leaving its more cynical, weathered spokesman to carry on. Surely this bitter irony was not lost on the aging Emerson.

◆ ◆ ◆

A word or two should be said about this compilation and my own biases. I have intentionally avoided Emerson's poetry because prose was, I believe, his greatest strength. Much of Emerson's writing dealt with history, biography, and religion — most of which I also avoided, focusing instead upon nature-related material. I leave it to others to compile more comprehensive selections of Emerson's work.

The excerpts presented here have been culled with an eye towards Emerson's unique worldview or to illustrate his own direct engagement with the wild. As Whitman said of Emerson and the organizations that he embraced at one time or another, "They never could hold him; no province, no clique, no church." After reading Richardson's biography of Emerson, I have become a convert to this view. There were only two constants in Emerson's life and work: an abiding desire to know the truth about the world, and an unwavering belief that truth is self-evident in nature. Anyone who delves deeply into Emerson must acknowledge this much, even if his wildness remains in doubt.

Walt McLaughlin
May 2006

Journals
1820–1836

Between his undergraduate studies at Harvard College and the publication of Nature, *Emerson cultivated a philosophy deeply rooted in the natural world. His early journal entries reflect this development. They also reveal an inclination towards fiercely independent thought, which ultimately led to his rejection of the ministry and the commencement of his lifelong work as both a writer and lecturer. In these journal fragments, we see a practical mind at work, heavily influenced by day-to-day realities.*

◆ ◆ ◆

I have often found cause to complain that my thoughts have an ebb and flow. Whether any laws fix them, and what the laws are, I cannot ascertain. I have quoted a thousand times the memory of Milton and tried to bind my thinking season to one part of the year, or to one sort of weather; to the sweet influence of the Pleiades, or to the summer reign of Lyra. The worst is, that the ebb is certain, long and frequent, while the flow comes transiently and seldom.

They say there is a tune which is forbidden to be played in the European armies because it makes the Swiss desert, since it reminds them so forcibly of their hills and home. I have heard many *Swiss tunes* played in college. Balancing between getting and not getting a hard lesson, a breath of fragrant air from the fields coming in at the window would serve as a Swiss tune and make me desert to the glens from which it came.

Why has my motley diary no jokes? Because it is a soliloquy and every man is grave alone.

I have heard a clergyman of Maine say that in his Parish are the Penobscot Indians, and that when any one of them in summer has been absent for some weeks a-hunting, he comes back among them a different person and altogether unlike any of the rest, with an eagle's eye, a wild look, and commanding carriage and gesture; but after a few weeks it wears off again into the indolent dronelike apathy which all exhibit.

The old fable said Truth was by gods or men made naked. I wish the gods would help her to a garment or make her fairer. From Eden to America the apples of the tree of knowledge are but bitter fruit in the end.

It is a peculiarity (I find by observation upon others) of humor in me, my strong propensity for strolling. I deliberately shut up my books in a cloudy July noon, put on my old clothes and old hat and slink away to the whortleberry bushes and slip with the greatest satisfaction into a little cowpath where I am sure I can defy observation. This point gained, I solace myself for hours with picking blueberries and other trash of the woods, far from fame, behind the birch-trees. I seldom enjoy hours as I do these. I remember them in winter; I expect them in spring.+

The year is long enough for all that is to be done in it. The flowers blow; the fruit ripens; and every species of animals [*sic*] is satisfied and attains its perfection, but man does not; man has seen more than he has had time to do.

The sun shines and warms and lights us and we have no curiosity to know why this is so; but we ask the reason of all evil, of pain, and hunger, and musquitoes [*sic*] and silly people.

If a man loves the city, so will his writings love the city, and if a man loves sweet fern and roams much in the pastures, his writings will smell of it.

The Religion that is afraid of science dishonours God and commits suicide.

A lobster is monstrous, but when we have been shown the reason of the case and the colour and the tentacula and the proportion of the claws, and seen that he has not a scale nor a bristle nor any quality but fits some habit and condition of the creature, he then seems as perfect and suitable to his sea-house as a glove to a hand. A man in the rocks under the sea would be a monster, but a lobster is a most handy and happy fellow there.

Blind men in Rome complained that the streets were dark. To the dull mind all nature is leaden. To the illuminated mind the whole world burns and sparkles with light.

Every popinjay blows with the wind. The thunder cloud sails against it.

Conway, N.H. Here among the mountains, the pinions of thought should be strong, and one should see the errors of men from a calmer height of love and wisdom.

The good of going into the mountains is that life is reconsidered; it is far from the slavery of your own modes of living, and you have [the] opportunity of viewing the town at such a distance as may afford you a just view, nor can you have any such mistaken apprehension as might be expected from the place you occupy and the round of customs you run at home.

The truth of truth consists in this, that it is self-evident, self-subsistent. It is light. You don't get a candle to see the sun rise.

I like the sayers of No better than the sayers of Yes.

Here we are impressed with the inexhaustible riches of nature. The universe is a more amazing puzzle than ever, as you glance along this bewildering series of animated forms, — the hazy butterflies, the carved shells, the birds, beasts, fishes, insects, snakes, and the upheaving principle of life everywhere

incipient, in the very rock aping organized forms. Not a form so grotesque, so savage, nor so beautiful but is an expression of some property inherent in man the observer, — an occult relation between the very scorpions and man. I feel the centipede in me, — cayman, carp, eagle, and fox. I am moved by strange sympathies; I say continually "I will be a naturalist."

I like my book about Nature, and wish I knew where and how I ought to live. God will show me.

When a man goes into the woods he feels like a boy without loss of wisdom. To be sure a dandy may go there, and Nature will never speak to a dandy.

See the perpetual generation of good sense: nothing wholly false, fantastic, can take possession of men who, to live and move, must plough the ground, sail the sea, have orchards, hear the robin sing, and see the swallow fly.

I remember when I was a boy going upon the beach and being charmed with the colors and forms of the shells. I picked up many and put them in my pocket. When I got home I could find nothing that I gathered — nothing but some dry, ugly mussel and snail shells. Thence I learned that composition was more important than the beauty of individual forms to effect.

The Muses love the woods, and I have come hither to court the awful Powers in this sober solitude. Whatsoever is highest, wisest, best, favor me! I will listen and then speak.

The Laws of Nature

Rain, rain. The good rain, like a bad preacher, does not know when to leave off.

I saw a hawk to-day wheeling up to heaven in a spiral flight, and every circle becoming less to the eye till he vanished into the atmosphere. What could be more in unison with all pure and brilliant images. Yet is the creature an unclean greedy eater, and all his geography from that grand observatory was a watching of barn-yards, or an inspection of moles and field-mice.

Many eyes go through the meadow, but few see the flowers in it.

No art can exceed the mellow beauty of one square rod of ground in the woods this afternoon. The noise of the locust, the bee, and the pine; the light, the insect forms, butterflies, cankerworms hanging, balloon-spiders swinging, devils-needles cruising, chirping grasshoppers; the tints and forms of the leaves and trees, — not a flower but its form seems a type, not a capsule but is an elegant seedbox, — then the myriad asters, polygalas, and golden-rods, and through the bush the far pines, and overhead the eternal sky.

I rejoice in Time. I do not cross the common without a wild poetic delight, notwithstanding the prose of my demeanour. Thank God I live in the country.

Every involuntary repulsion that arises in your mind, give heed unto. It is the surface of a central truth.

The maker of a sentence launches out into the infinite and builds a road into Chaos and old Night, and is followed by those who hear him with something of wild, creative delight.

Who can tell the moment when the pine outgrew the whortleberry that shaded its first sprout. It went by in the night.

A wonderful sight is the inverted landscape. Look at the prospect from a high hill through your legs, and it gives the world a most pictorial appearance.

We cross the ocean sweltering, sea-sick, reeling, week after week, with tar, harness-tub, and bilge, and, as an ingenious friend says, it is carrying the joke too far.

Society seems noxious. I believe that against these baleful influences Nature is the antidote. The man comes out of the wrangle of the shop and office, and sees the sky and the woods, and is a man again. He not only quits the cabal, but he finds himself. But how few men see the sky and the woods!

If I study an ant-hill and neglect all business, all history, all conversation, yet shall that ant-hill, humbly and lovingly and unceasingly explored, furnish me with a parallel experience and the same conclusions to which business, history and conversation would have brought me.

I gladly pay the rent of my house because I therewith get the horizon and the woods which I pay no rent for. For daybreak and evening and night, I pay no tax. I think it is a glorious bargain which I drive with the town.

Poverty, Frost, Famine, Rain, Disease, are the beadles and guardsmen that hold us to Common Sense.

For form's sake, or for wantonness, I sometimes chaffer with the farmer on the price of a cord of wood, but if he said twenty dollars instead of five, I should think it cheap when I remember the beautiful botanical wonder — the bough of an oak — which he brings me so freely out of the enchanted forest where the sun and water, air and earth and God formed it.

Excerpts from *Nature*

In his slender book, Nature, *Emerson outlined a philosophy that would soon be known as American Transcendentalism — a curious fusion of European Idealism and Romanticism with Yankee common sense. More to the point, Emerson shows in this book how any discourse on truth, God, or reality is essentially an inquiry into the natural world. Even human nature is but a facet of nature. Hence, a thorough understanding of the laws of nature is key to understanding everything else. Truth, love, morality, beauty, the physical world — it all comes together in nature.*

◆ ◆ ◆

The foregoing generations beheld God and nature face to face; we, through their eyes. Why should not we also enjoy an original relation to the universe? Why should not we have a poetry and philosophy of insight and not of tradition, and a religion by revelation to us, and not the history of theirs? Embosomed for a season in nature, whose floods of life stream around and through us, and invite us by the powers they supply, to action proportioned to nature, why should we grope among the dry bones of the past, or put the living generation into masquerade out of its faded wardrobe? The sun shines to-day also.

All science has one aim, namely, to find a theory of nature. We have theories of races and of functions, but scarcely yet a remote approximation to an idea of creation.

To go into solitude, a man needs to retire as much from his chamber as from society. I am not solitary whilst I read and write, though nobody is with me. But if a man would be alone, let him look at the stars. The rays that come from those heavenly worlds, will separate between him and vulgar things.

The stars awaken a certain reverence, because though always present, they are always inaccessible; but all natural objects make a kindred impression, when the mind is open to their influence.

A lover of nature is he whose inward and outward senses are still truly adjusted to each other; who has retained the spirit of infancy even into the era of manhood. His intercourse with heaven and earth, becomes part of his daily food. In the presence of nature, a wild delight runs through the man, in spite of real sorrows.

The greatest delight which the fields and woods minister, is the suggestion of an occult relation between man and the vegetable. I am not alone and unacknowledged. They nod to me and I to them.

The misery of man appears like childish petulance, when we explore the steady and prodigal provision that has been made for his support and delight on this green ball which floats him through the heavens.

The health of the eye seems to demand a horizon. We are never tired, so long as we can see far enough.

How does Nature deify us with a few and cheap elements! Give me health and a day, and I will make the pomp of emperors ridiculous.

The Laws of Nature

To the attentive eye, each moment of the year has its own beauty, and in the same field, it beholds, every hour, a picture which was never seen before, and which shall never be seen again.

Go out of the house to see the moon, and 't is mere tinsel; it will not please as when its light shines upon your necessary journey. The beauty that shimmers in the yellow afternoons of October, who ever could clutch it? Go forth to find it, and it is gone: 't is only a mirage as you look from the windows of diligence.

Beauty is the mark God sets upon virtue. Every natural action is graceful. Every heroic act is also decent, and causes the place and the bystanders to shine. We are taught by great actions that the universe is the property of every individual in it. Every rational creature has all nature for his dowry and estate.

In private places, among sordid objects, an act of truth or heroism seems at once to draw to itself the sky as its temple, the sun as its candle. Nature stretcheth out her arms to embrace man, only let his thoughts be of equal greatness.

Nothing divine dies. All good is eternally reproductive. The beauty of nature reforms itself in the mind, and not for barren contemplation, but for new creation.

Nature, in its ministry to man, is not only the material, but is also the process and the result.

Nature is a sea of forms radically alike and even unique. A leaf, a sun-beam, a landscape, the ocean, make an analogous impression on the mind. What is common to them all, — that perfectness and harmony, is beauty.

Beauty, in its largest and profoundest sense, is one expression for the universe. God is the all-fair. Truth, and goodness, and beauty, are but different faces of the same All.

Every natural fact is a symbol of some spiritual fact. Every appearance in nature corresponds to some state of the mind, and that state of the mind can only be described by presenting that natural appearance as its picture.

Who looks upon a river in a meditative hour, and is not reminded of the flux of all things? Throw a stone into the stream, and the circles that propagate themselves are the beautiful type of all influence.

Hundreds of writers may be found in every long-civilized nation, who for a short time believe, and make others believe, that they see and utter truths, who do not of themselves clothe one thought in its natural garment, but who feed unconsciously upon the language created by the primary writers of the country, those, namely, who hold primarily to nature.

All the facts in natural history taken by themselves, have no value, but are barren like a single sex. But marry it to human history, and it is full of life.

We know more from nature than we can at will communicate. Its light flows into the mind evermore, and we forget its presence.

Have mountains, and waves, and skies, no significance but what we consciously give them, when we employ them as emblems of our thoughts? The world is emblematic. Parts of speech are metaphors because the whole of nature is a metaphor of the human mind. The laws of moral nature answer to those of matter as face to face in a glass.

A Fact is the end or last issue of spirit. The visible creation is the terminus or the circumference of the invisible world.

A life in harmony with nature, the love of truth and of virtue, will purge the eyes to understand her text. By degrees we may come to know the primitive sense of the permanent objects of nature, so that the world shall be to us an open book, and every form significant of its hidden life and final cause.

Space, time, society, labor, climate, food, locomotion, the animals, the mechanical forces, give us sincerest lessons, day by day, whose meaning is unlimited. They educate both the Understanding and the Reason.

Water is good to drink, coal to burn, wool to wear; but wool cannot be drunk, nor water spun, nor coal eaten. The wise man shows his wisdom in separation, in gradation, and his scale of creatures and of merits, is as wide as nature.

The first steps in Agriculture, Astronomy, Zoology, (those first steps which the farmer, the hunter, and the sailor take,) teach that nature's dice are always loaded; that in her heaps and rubbish are concealed sure and useful results.

How calmly and genially the mind apprehends one after another the laws of physics! What noble emotions dilate the mortal as he enters into the counsels of the creation, and feels by knowledge the privilege to Be!

Nothing in nature is exhausted in its first use. When a thing has served an end to the uttermost, it is wholly new for an ulterior service. In God, every end is converted into a new means.

The moral law lies at the centre of nature and radiates to the circumference. It is the pith and marrow of every substance, every relation, and every process. All things with which we deal, preach to us.

The moral influence of nature upon every individual is that amount of truth which it illustrates to him. Who can estimate this? Who can guess how much firmness the sea-beaten rock has taught the fisherman? how much tranquillity has been reflected to man from the azure sky, over whose unspotted deeps the winds forevermore drive flocks of stormy clouds, and leave no wrinkle or stain? how much industry and providence and affection we have caught from the pantomime of brutes?

But whilst we acquiesce entirely in the permanence of natural laws, the question of the absolute existence of nature, still remains open.

The river, as it flows, resembles the air that flows over it; the air resembles the light which traverses it with more subtile currents; the light resembles the heat which rides with it through Space. Each creature is only a modification of the other; the likeness in them is more than the difference, and their radical law is one and the same. Hence it is, that a rule of one art, or a law of one organization, holds true throughout nature.

The frivolous make themselves merry with the Ideal theory, as if its consequences were burlesque; as if it affected the stability of nature. It surely does not. God never jests with us, and will not compromise the end of nature, by permitting any inconsequence in its procession.

If the Reason be stimulated to more earnest vision, outlines and surfaces become transparent, and are no longer seen; causes and spirits are seen through them. The best, the happiest moments of life, are these delicious awakenings of the higher powers, and the reverential withdrawing of nature before its God.

Nature is made to conspire with spirit to emancipate us.

The sensual man conforms thoughts to things; the poet conforms things to his thoughts. The one esteems nature as rooted and fast; the other, as fluid, and impresses his being thereon.

Whilst thus the poet delights us by animating nature like a creator, with his own thoughts, he differs from the philosopher only herein, that the one proposes Beauty as his main end; the other Truth.

The true philosopher and the true poet are one, and a beauty, which is truth, and a truth, which is beauty, is the aim of both.

Idealism is a hypothesis to account for nature by other principles than those of carpentry and chemistry. Yet, if it only deny the existence of matter, it does not satisfy the demands of the spirit. It leaves God out of me. It leaves me in a splendid labyrinth of my perceptions, to wander without end.

As a plant upon the earth, so a man rests upon the bosom of God; he is nourished by unfailing fountains, and draws, at his need, inexhaustible power.

We are as much strangers in nature, as we are aliens from God. We do not understand the notes of birds. The fox and the deer run away from us; the bear and tiger rend us. We do not know the uses of more than a few plants, as corn and the apple, the potato and the vine. Is not the landscape, every glimpse of which hath a grandeur, a face of him?

The savant becomes unpoetic. But the best read naturalist who lends an entire and devout attention to truth, will see that there remains much to learn of his relation to the world, and that it is not to be learned by any addition or subtraction or other comparison of known quantities, but is arrived at by untaught sallies of the spirit, by a continual self-recovery, and by entire humility.

When I behold a rich landscape, it is less to my purpose to recite correctly the order and superposition of the strata, than to know why all thought of multitude is lost in a tranquil sense of unity.

At present, man applies to nature but half his force. He works on the world with his understanding alone. He lives in it, and masters it by a penny-wisdom; and he that works most in it, is but a half-man, and whilst his arms are strong and his digestion good, his mind is imbruted and he is a selfish savage.

The problem of restoring to the world original and eternal beauty, is solved by the redemption of the soul. The ruin or the blank, that we see when we look at nature, is in our own eye.

The invariable mark of wisdom is to see the miraculous in the common.

Whilst the abstract question occupies your intellect, nature brings it in the concrete to be solved by your hands.

Journals
1837–1844

Emerson came into his own as a thinker, lecturer, and writer in the late 1830s and early 1840s. He made his final break with organized religion, edited a literary journal called The Dial *with Margaret Fuller, and wrote two volumes of essays during this period. He also became friends with Henry David Thoreau, with whom he shared a deep affinity for nature. This was a mutually beneficial friendship that fanned the intellectual fires burning within both men. Despite this cross-pollination, we find a depth and breadth in Emerson's reflections on nature that indicate an exceptionally active mind, influenced by direct encounter with the wild itself.*

◆ ◆ ◆

How wild and mysterious our position as individuals to the Universe. We understand nothing; our ignorance is abysmal, the overhanging immensity staggers us, whither we go, what we do, who we are, we cannot even so much as guess. We stagger and grope.

I see with joy the visits of heat and moisture to my trees, and please myself with this new property. I strangely mix myself with nature, and the Universal God works, buds, and blooms in my grove and parterre. I seem to myself an enchanter who by some rune or dumb-gesture compels the service of superior beings. But the instant I separate *my own* from the tree and the potato field, it loses this piquancy. I presently see that I also am an instrument like the tree, a reagent. The tree was to grow; I was to transplant and water it, not for me, not for it, but for all.

Yesterday in the woods I followed the fine humble bee with rhymes and fancies fine.

I believe I shall some time cease to be an individual, that the eternal tendency of the soul is to become Universal, to animate the last extremities of organization.

Nature still solicits me. Overhead the sanctities of the stars shine forevermore, and to me also, pouring satire on the pompous business of the day which they close, and making the generations of men show slight and evanescent. A man is but a bug, the earth but a boat, a cockle, drifting under their old light.

'Miracles have ceased.' Have they indeed? When? They had not ceased this afternoon when I walked into the wood and got into bright, miraculous sunshine, in shelter from the roaring wind.

February 17, 1838. My good Henry Thoreau made this else solitary afternoon sunny with his simplicity and clear perception. How comic is simplicity in this double-dealing, quacking world. Everything that boy says makes merry with society, though nothing can be graver than his meaning.

I am agitated with curiosity to know the secret of nature. Why cannot geology, why cannot botany speak and tell me what has been, what is, as I run along the forest promontory, and ask when it rose like a blister on heated steel? Then I looked up and saw the sun shining in the vast sky, and heard the wind bellow above and the water glistened in the vale. These were the forces that wrought then and work now. Yes, there they grandly speak to all plainly, in proportion as we are quick to apprehend.

Last night ill dreams. Dreams are true to nature and, like monstrous formations (e.g. the horse-hoof divided into toes), show the law.

It is very hard to be simple enough to be good.

Yesterday afternoon I went to the Cliff with Henry Thoreau. Warm, pleasant, misty weather, which the great mountain amphitheatre seemed to drink in with gladness. A crow's voice filled all the miles of air with sound. A bird's voice, even a piping frog, enlivens a solitude and makes world enough for us. At night I went out into the dark and saw a glimmering star and heard a frog, and Nature seemed to say, Well, do not these suffice? Here is a new scene, a new experience. Ponder it, Emerson, and not like the foolish world, hanker after thunders and multitudes and vast landscapes, the sea or Niagara.

Astronomy is sedative to the human mind. In skeptical hours when things go whirling and we doubt if all is not an extemporary dream: the calm, remote and secular character of astronomical facts composes us to a sublime peace.

Last night the moon rose behind four distinct pine-tree tops in the distant woods and the night at ten was so bright that I walked abroad. But the sublime light of night is unsatisfying, provoking; it astonishes but explains not. Its charm floats, dances, disappears, comes and goes, but palls in five minutes after you have left the house. Come out of your warm, angular house, resounding with few voices, into the chill, grand, instantaneous night, with such a Presence as a full moon in the clouds, and you are struck with poetic wonder. In the instant

you leave far behind all human relations, wife, mother and child, and live only with the savages — water, air, light, carbon, lime, and granite. I become a moist, cold element. "Nature grows over me." Frogs pipe; waters far off tinkle; dry leaves hiss; grass bends and rustles, and I have died out of the human world and come to feel a strange, cold, aqueous, terraqueous, aerial, ethereal sympathy and existence. I sow the sun and moon for seeds.

A man must have aunts and cousins, must buy carrots and turnips, must have barn and woodshed, must go to market and to the blacksmith's shop, must saunter and sleep and be inferior and silly.

In the wood, God was manifest, as he was not in the sermon. In the cathedralled larches the ground-pine crept him, the thrush sung him, the robin complained him, the cat-bird mewed him, the anemone vibrated him, the wild apple bloomed him; the ants built their little Timbuctoo wide abroad; the wild grape budded; the rye was in the blade; high overhead, high over cloud, the faint, sharp-horned moon sailed steadily west through fleets of little clouds; the sheaves of the birch brightened into green below. The pines kneaded their aromatics in the sun. All prepared itself for the warm thunder-days of July.

Why do we seek this lurking beauty in skies, in poems, in drawings? Ah! because there we are safe, there we neither sicken nor die. I think we fly to Beauty as an asylum from the terrors of finite nature. We are made immortal by this kiss, by the contemplation of beauty.

The moon and Jupiter side by side last night stemmed the sea of clouds and plied their voyage in convoy through the sublime Deep as I walked the old and dusty road. The snow and the enchantment of the moonlight make all landscapes alike, and the road that is so tedious and homely that I never take it by day, — by night is Italy or Palmyra. In these divine pleasures permitted to me of walks in the June night under moon and stars, I can put my life as a fact before me and stand aloof from its honor and shame.

We came home, Elizabeth Hoar and I, at night from Waltham. The moon and stars and night wind made coolness and tranquillity grateful after the crowd and the festival. Elizabeth, in Lincoln woods, said that the woods always looked as if they waited whilst you passed by — waited for you to be gone.

Read and think. Study now, and now garden. Go alone, then go abroad. Speculate awhile, then work in the world.

Trees look to me like imperfect men. It is the same soul that makes me, which, by a feebler effort, arrives at these graceful portraits of life. I think we all feel so. I think we all feel a certain pity in beholding a tree: rooted there, the would-be-Man is beautiful, but patient and helpless. His boughs and long leaves droop and weep his strait imprisonment.

What makers are our eyes! In yonder boat on the pond the two boys, no doubt, find prose enough. Yet to us, as we sit here on the shore, it is quite another sort of canoe, a piece of fairy timber which the light loves and the wind, and the wave, — a piece of sunshine and beauty.

After thirty, a man is too sensible of the strait limitations which his physical constitution sets to his activity. The stream feels its banks, which it had forgotten in the run and overflow of the first meadows.

Books. — It seems meritorious to read: but from everything but history or the works of the old commanding writers I come back with a conviction that the slightest *wood-thought*, the least significant native emotion of my own, is more to me.

Nature is the beautiful asylum to which we look in all the years of striving and conflict as the assured resource when we shall be driven out of society by ennui or chagrin or persecution or defect of character.

Nature is no fool. She knows the world. She has calculated the chances of her success, and if her seeds do not vegetate, she will not be chagrined and bereft. She has another arrow left, another card to play, her harvest is insured. From her oak she scatters down a thousand seeds, and if nine hundred rot, the forest is still perpetuated for a century.

Every man's idea of God is the last or most comprehensive generalization at which he has arrived.

> *It is a beautiful fact that every spot of earth, every dog, pebble, and ash-heap, as well as every palace and every man, is whirled around in turn to the meridian.*

Steady, steady! When this fog of good and evil affections falls, it is hard to see and walk straight.

My brave Henry Thoreau walked with me to Walden this afternoon and complained of the proprietors who compelled him, to whom, as much as to any, the whole world belonged, to walk in a strip of road and crowded him out of all the rest of God's earth. I begged him, having this maggot of Freedom and Humanity in his brain, to write it out into good poetry and so clear himself of it.

In the morning a man walks with his whole body; in the evening, only with his legs; the trunk is carried along almost motionless.

I like the rare, extravagant spirits who disclose to me new facts in nature.

Races pass and perish; cities rise and fall, like the perpetual succession of shells on the beach; and the sound of the waters and the colors of the flower, cloud, and the voice of man are as new and affecting today as at any moment in the vast Past.

July 20. Night in this enchanting season is not night, but a miscellany of lights. The journeying twilight, the half-moon, the kindling Venus, the beaming Jove, — Saturn and Mars something less bright, and, fainter still, 'the common people of the sky,' as Crashaw said: then, below, the meadows and thickets flashing with the fireflies, and all around the farms the steadier lamps of men compose the softest, warmest illumination.

I see my thought standing, growing, walking, working, out there in nature. Look where I will, I see it. Yet when I seek to say it, all men say, "No: it is not. These are whimsies and dreams!" Then I think they look at one thing, and I at others. My thoughts, though not false, are far, as yet, from simple truth, and I am rebuked by their disapprobation, nor think of questioning it. Society is yet too great for me.

My life is a May game, I will live as I like. I defy your strait-laced, weary social ways and modes. Blue is the sky; green the fields and groves, fresh the springs, glad the rivers, and hospitable the splendor of sun and star. I will play my game out.

When I walk in Walden wood, as on 4 July, I seem to myself an inexhaustible poet, if only I could once break through the fence of silence, and vent myself in adequate rhyme.

Nature delights in punishing stupid people. The very strawberry vines are more than a match for them with all their appetites, and all their fumbling fingers. The little, defenceless vine coolly hides the best berry, now under this leaf, then under that, and keeps the treasure for yonder darling boy with the bright eyes when Booby is gone.

A walk in the woods is only an exalted dream.

We are shut up in schools and college recitation rooms for ten or fifteen years, and come out at last with a bellyful of words and do not know a thing. We cannot use our hands, or our legs, or our eyes, or our arms. We do not know an edible root in the woods. We cannot tell our course by the stars,

nor the hour of the day by the sun. It is well if we can swim and skate. We are afraid of a horse, of a cow, of a dog, of a cat, of a spider. Far better was the Roman rule to teach a boy nothing that he could not learn standing.

In the country, the lover of nature dreaming through the wood would never awake to thought if the scream of an eagle, the cries of a crow or a curlew near his head, did not break the continuity.

The Laws of Nature

It is the condition of inspiration — Marry Nature, and not use her for pleasure.

As the wandering sea-bird which, crossing the ocean, alights on some rock or islet to rest for a moment its wings and to look back on the wilderness of waves behind and forward to the wilderness of waters before, so stand we perched on this rock or shoal of Time arrived out of the Immensity of the Past and bound and road-ready to plunge into immensity again.

Did you ever eat the poorest rye or oatcake with a beautiful maiden in the wilderness? and did you not find that the mixture of sun and sky with your bread gave it a certain mundane savour and comeliness?

There are, no doubt, many dogs barking at the moon, and many owls hooting in this Saturday night of the world, but the fair moon knows nothing of either.

We walked this afternoon to Edmund Hosmer's and Walden Pond. The South wind blew and filled with bland and warm light the dry sunny woods. The last year's leaves flew like birds through the air. As I sat on the bank of the Drop, or God's Pond, and saw the amplitude of the little water, what space, what verge, the little scudding fleets of ripples found to scatter and spread from side to side and take so much time to cross the pond, and saw how the water seemed made for the wind, and the wind for the water, dear playfellows for each other, — I said to my companion, I declare this world is so beautiful that I can hardly believe it exists.

Beware when the great God lets loose a new thinker on this planet.

I went into the woods. I found myself not wholly present there. If I looked at a pine-tree or an aster, *that* did not seem to be Nature. Nature was still elsewhere: this, or this was but outskirt and far-off reflection and echo of the triumph that had passed by and was now at its glancing splendor and heyday, — perchance in the neighboring fields, or, if I stood in the field, then in the adjacent woods. Always the present object gave me this sense of the stillness that follows a pageant that has just gone by.

The books of men of genius are divers or dippers. When they alight on the water, they soon disappear, but after some space they emerge again. Other books are land-birds which, falling in the water, know well that their own safety is in keeping at the top. They flutter and chirp and scream, but if they once get their heads under they are drowned forever.

Every hour has its morning, noon, and night.

An apple-tree near at hand is a great awkward flower, but seen at some distance it gives a wonderful softness to the landscape.

I love spring water and wild air, and not the manufacture of the chemist's shop. I see in a moment, on looking into our new *Dial*, which is the wild poetry, and which the tame, and see that one wild line out of a private heart saves the whole book.

The pastures are full of ghosts for me, the morning woods full of angels. Now and then they give me a broad hint.

When I look at the sweeping sleet amid the pine woods, my sentences look very contemptible, and I think I will never write more: but the words prompted by an irresistible charity, the words whose path from the heart to the lips I cannot follow, — are fairer than the snow. It is pitiful to be an artist. …

Pirates do not live on nuts and herbs.

I am sometimes discontented with my house because it lies on a dusty road, and with its sills and cellar almost in the water of the meadow. But when I creep out of it into the Night or the Morning and see what majestic and what tender beauties daily wrap me in their bosom, how near to me is every transcendent secret of Nature's love and religion, I see how indifferent it is where I eat and sleep.

Coffee is good for talent, but genius wants prayer.

The good river-god has taken the form of my valiant Henry Thoreau here and introduced me to the riches of his shadowy, starlit, moonlit stream, a lovely new world lying as close and yet as unknown to this vulgar trite one of streets and shops as death to life, or poetry to prose. Through one field only we went to the boat and then left all time, all science, all history, behind us, and entered into Nature with one stroke of a paddle.

The turnip grows in the same soil with the strawberry; knows all the nourishment that it gets, and feeds on the very same itself, yet is a turnip still.

Beauty can never be clutched.

Lotus-eaters. I suppose there is no more abandoned epicure or opium-eater than I. I taste every hour of these autumn days. Every light from the sky, every shadow on earth, ministers to my pleasure. I love this gas. I grudge to move or to labor or to change my book or to will, lest I should disturb the sweet dream.

I see the law of Nature equally exemplified in bar-room and in a saloon of philosophers.

On this wonderful day when Heaven and Earth seem to glow with magnificence, and all the wealth of all the elements is put under contribution to make the world fine, as if Nature would indulge her offspring, it seemed ungrateful to hide in the house. Are there not dull days enough in the year for you to write and read in, that you should waste this glittering season when Florida and Cuba seem to have left their seats and come to visit us, with all their shining Hours, and almost we expect to see the jasmine and the cactus burst from the ground instead of these last gentians and asters which have loitered to attend this latter glory of the year? All insects are out, all birds come forth, — the very cattle that lie on the ground seem to have great thoughts, and Egypt and India look from their eyes.

Young preachers are but chipping birds, who chirp now on the bushes, now on the ground, but do not mean anything by their chirping.

There is truly but one miracle, the
perpetual fact of Being and Becoming,
the ceaseless saliency, the transit
from the Vast to the particular, which
miracle, one and the same, has for its
most universal name the word *God*.
Take one or two or three steps where
you will, from any fact in Nature or
Art, and you come out full on this
fact; as you may penetrate the forest in
any direction and go straight on, you
will come to the sea.

The Universe does not jest with us,
but is in earnest.

Last night a walk to the river
with Margaret, and saw the moon
broken in the water, interrogating,
interrogating.

Henry Thoreau made, last night, the fine remark that, as long as a man stands in his own way,
everything seems to be in his way, governments, society, and even the sun and moon and stars, as
astrology may testify.

Do not be too timid and squeamish about your actions. All life is an experiment. The more
experiments you make the better. What if they are a little coarse, and you may get your coat soiled
or torn? What if you do fail, and get fairly rolled in the dirt once or twice? Up again, you shall
never be so afraid of a tumble.

A poet may eat bread for his breakfast, and bread and flesh for his dinner, but for his supper he
must eat stars only.

The oak leaf is perfect, a kind of absolute realized, but every work of art is only relatively good;
— the artist advances, and finds all his fine things naught.

The Laws of Nature

Earth Spirit, living, a black river like that swarthy stream which rushes through the human body is thy nature, demoniacal, warm, fruitful, sad, nocturnal.

My garden is an honest place. Every tree and every vine are incapable of concealment, and tell after two or three months exactly what sort of treatment they have had. The sower may mistake and sow his peas crookedly: the peas make no mistake, but come up and show his line.

Mountains are great poets, and one glance at this fine cliff scene undoes a great deal of prose, and reinstates us wronged men in our rights. All life, all society begins to get illuminated and transparent, and we generalize boldly and well. Space is felt as a great thing.

Is life a thunderstorm that we can see now by a flash the whole horizon, and then cannot see our right hand?

The sky is the daily bread of the eyes. What sculpture in these hard clouds; what expression of immense amplitude in this dotted and rippled rack, here firm and continental, there vanishing into

The only straight line in Nature that I remember is the spider swinging down from a twig.

plumes and auroral gleams. No crowding; boundless, cheerful, and strong.

If I could freely and manly go to the mountains, or to the prairie, or to the sea, I would not hesitate for inconvenience: but to cart all my pots and kettles, kegs and clothespins, and all that belongs thereunto, over the mountains, seems not worth while. I should not be nearer to sun or star.

Henry Thoreau's conversation consisted of a continual coining of the present moment into a sentence and offering it to me. I compared it to a boy, who, from the universal snow lying on the earth, gathers up a little in his hand, rolls it into a ball, and flings it at me.

A rose, a sunbeam, the human face, do not remind us of deacons.

Excerpts from *Essays*
and
Essays, Second Series

Emerson's Essays *was published in 1841.* Essays, Second Series *appeared in 1844.*
Together these two collections constitute the core of Emersonian thought as most people
know it. Reprinted collections of his work usually derive from these two volumes. This is no
accident. Here is Emerson at his best: lucid, thoughtful, and poetic. Here, too, nature plays a
central role, as Emerson fleshes out his inexorable laws — the particulars of nature frequently
evolving into general conclusions.

◆ ◆ ◆

Nature is a mutable cloud which is always and never the same. She casts the same thoughts into troops of forms, as a poet makes twenty fables with one moral. Beautifully shines a spirit through the bruteness and toughness of matter. Nature is endless combination and repetition of a very few laws. She hums the old well known air through innumerable variations.

The Gothic church plainly originated in a rude adaptation of the forest trees, with all their boughs, to a festal or solemn arcade; as the bands about the cleft pillars still indicate the green withes that tied them. No one can walk in a road cut through pine woods, without being struck with the architectural appearance of the grove, especially in winter, when the barrenness of all other trees shows the low arch of the Saxons.

The man who has seen the rising moon break out of the clouds at midnight, has been present like an archangel at the creation of light and of the world.

Some men have so much of the Indian left, have constitutionally such habits of accommodation that at sea, or in the forest, or in the snow, they sleep as warm, and dine with as good appetite, and associate as happily as in their own house.

The power of man consists in the multitude of his affinities, in the fact that his life is intertwined with the whole chain of organic and inorganic being.

In this pleasing contrite wood-life which God allows me, let me record day by day my honest thought without prospect or retrospect, and, I cannot doubt, it will be found symmetrical, though I mean it not and see it not. My book should smell of pines and resound with the hum of insects. The swallow over my window should interweave that thread or straw he carries in his bill into my web also.

Let us affront and reprimand the smooth mediocrity and squalid contentment of the times, and hurl in the face of custom and trade and office, the fact which is the upshot of all history, that there is a great responsible Thinker and Actor moving wherever moves a man; that a true man belongs to no other time or place, but is the centre of things. Where he is, there is nature.

A foolish consistency is the hobgoblin of little minds,
adored by little statesmen and philosophers and divines.

Before a leaf-bud has burst, its whole life acts; in the full-blown flower there is no more; in the leafless root there is no less. Its nature is satisfied and it satisfies nature in all moments alike. There is no time to it. But man postpones or remembers; he does not live in the present, but with reverted eye laments the past, or, heedless of the riches that surround him, stands on tiptoe to foresee the future. He cannot be happy and strong until he too lives with nature in the present, above time.

Every thing in nature contains all the powers of nature. Every thing is made of one hidden stuff; as the naturalist sees one type under every metamorphosis, and regards a horse as a running man, a fish as a swimming man, a bird as a flying man, a tree as a rooted man. Each new form repeats not only the main character of the type, but part for part all the details, all the aims, furtherances, hindrances, energies and whole system of every other.

The dice of God are always loaded. The world looks like a multiplication-table, or a mathematical equation, which, turn it how you will, balances itself.

Our action is overmastered and characterized above our will by the law of nature. We aim at a petty end quite aside from the public good, but our act arranges itself by irresistible magnetism in a line with the poles of the world.

If you are wise you will dread a prosperity which only loads you with more. Benefit is the end of nature. But for every benefit which you receive, a tax is levied.

Commit a crime, and it seems as if a coat of snow fell on the ground, such as reveals in the woods the track of every partridge and fox and squirrel and mole. You cannot recall the spoken word, you cannot wipe out the foot-track, you cannot draw up the ladder, so as to leave no inlet or clew. Always some damning circumstance transpires. The laws and substances of nature, water, snow, wind, gravitation, become penalties to the thief.

There is no penalty to virtue; no penalty to wisdom; they are proper additions of being. In a virtuous action I properly *am*; in a virtuous act I add to the world; I plant into deserts conquered from Chaos and Nothing and see darkness receding on the limits of the horizon. There can be no excess to love, none to knowledge, none to beauty, when these attributes are considered in the purest sense.

The history of persecution is a history of endeavors to cheat nature, to make water run up hill, to twist a rope of sand. It makes no difference whether the actors be many or one, a tyrant or a mob.

Nature will not have us fret and fume. She does not like our benevolence or our learning much better than she likes our frauds and wars. When we come out of the caucus, or the bank, or the Abolition Convention, or the Temperance meeting, or the Transcendental club into the fields and woods, she says to us, "So hot? my little sir."

Let us draw a lesson from nature, which always works by short ways. When the fruit is ripe, it falls. When the fruit is despatched, the leaf falls. The circuit of the waters is mere falling. The walking of man and all animals is a falling forward. All our manual labor and works of strength, as prying, splitting, digging, rowing and so forth, are done by dint of continual falling, and the globe, earth, moon, comet, sun, star, fall forever and ever.

A little consideration of what takes place around us every day would show us that a higher law than that of our will regulates events; that our painful labors are very unnecessary and altogether fruitless; that only in our easy, simple, spontaneous action are we strong, and by contenting ourselves with obedience we become divine.

There is a soul at the centre of nature and over the will of every man, so that none of us can wrong the universe.

We can love nothing but nature. The most wonderful talents, the most meritorious exertions really avail very little with us; but nearness or likeness of nature, — how beautiful is the ease of its victory!

Truth has not single victories: all things are its organs, not only dust and stones, but errors and lies. The laws of disease, physicians say, are as beautiful as the laws of health. Our philosophy is affirmative and readily accepts the testimony of negative facts, as every shadow points to the sun. By a divine necessity every fact in nature is constrained to offer its testimony.

Every soul is a celestial Venus to every other soul. The heart has its sabbaths and jubilees in which the world appears as a hymeneal feast, and all natural sounds and the circle of the seasons are erotic odes and dances. Love is omnipresent in nature as motive and reward.

The Laws of Nature

Behold there in the wood the fine madman! He is a palace of sweet sounds and sights; he dilates; he is twice a man; he walks with arms akimbo; he soliloquizes; he accosts the grass and trees; he feels the blood of the violet, the clover and the lily in his veins; and he talks with the brook that wets his foot.

We cannot get at beauty. Its nature is like opaline doves'-neck lustres, hovering and evanescent. Herein it resembles the most excellent things, which all have this rainbow character, defying all attempts at appropriation and use.

Our friendships hurry to short and poor conclusions, because we have made them a texture of wine and dreams, instead of the tough fibre of the human heart. The laws of friendship are great, austere and eternal, of one web with the laws of nature and of morals.

I do not wish to treat friendships daintily, but with roughest courage. When they are real, they are not glass threads or frost-work, but the solidest thing we know.

Should not the society of my friend be to me poetic, pure, universal and great as nature itself? Ought I to feel that our tie is profane in comparison with yonder bar of cloud that sleeps on the horizon, or that clump of waving grass that divides the brook? Let us not vilify, but raise it to that standard.

The higher the style we demand of friendship, of course the less easy to establish it with flesh and blood.

Prudence does not go behind nature and ask whence it is? It takes the laws of the world whereby man's being is conditioned, as they are, and keeps these laws that it may enjoy their proper good. It respects space and time, climate, want, sleep, the law of polarity, growth and death.

Do what we can, summer will have its flies. If we walk in the woods we must feed mosquitos. If we go a-fishing we must expect a wet coat. Then climate is a great impediment to idle persons. We often resolve to give up the care of the weather, but still we regard the clouds and the rain.

Nature punishes any neglect of prudence. If you think the senses final, obey their law. If you believe in the soul, do not clutch at sensual sweetness before it is ripe on the slow tree of cause and effect.

Life is a festival only to the wise.

Man is a stream whose source is hidden. Always our being is descending into us from we know not whence.

We see the world piece by piece, as the sun, the moon, the animal, the tree; but the whole, of which these are the shining parts, is the soul.

We are often made to feel that there is another youth and age than that which is measured from the year of our natural birth. Some thoughts always find us young, and keep us so. Such a thought is the love of the universal and eternal beauty.

A thrill passes through all men at the reception of new truth, or at the performance of a great action, which comes out of the heart of nature.

The eye is the first circle; the horizon which it forms in the second; and throughout nature this primary picture is repeated without end. It is the highest emblem in the cipher of the world.

Our life is an apprenticeship to the truth that around every circle another can be drawn; that there is no end in nature, but every end is a beginning; that there is always another dawn risen on the mid-noon, and under every deep a lower deep opens.

Nature looks provokingly stable and secular, but it has a cause like all the rest; and when once I comprehend that, will these fields stretch so immovably wide, these leaves hang so individually considerable? Permanence is a word of degrees.

In nature every moment is new; the past is always swallowed and forgotten; the coming only is sacred. Nothing is secure but life, transition, the energizing spirit. No love can be bound by oath or covenant to secure it against a higher love. No truth so sublime but it may be trivial to-morrow in the light of new thoughts.

The natural world may be conceived of as a system of concentric circles, and we now and then detect in nature slight dislocations which apprize us that this surface on which we now stand is not fixed, but sliding.

God offers to every mind its choice between truth and repose. Take which you please, — you can never have both.

He who is immersed in what concerns person or place cannot see the problem of existence. This the intellect always ponders. Nature shows all things formed and bound. The intellect pierces the form, overleaps the wall, detects intrinsic likeness between remote things and reduces all things into a few principles.

All our progress is an unfolding, like the vegetable bud. You have first an instinct, then an opinion, then a knowledge, as the plant has root, bud and fruit.

We talk with accomplished persons who appear to be strangers in nature. The cloud, the tree, the turf, the bird, are not theirs, have nothing of them; the world is only their lodging and table. But the poet, whose verses are to be spheral and complete, is one whom nature cannot deceive, whatsoever face of strangeness she may put on. He feels a strict consanguinity, and detects more likeness than variety in all her changes.

What is man but a finer and compacter landscape than the horizon figures; nature's eclecticism? and what is his speech, his love of painting, love of nature, but a still finer success? all the weary miles and tons of space and bulk left out, and the spirit or moral of it contracted into a musical word, or the most cunning stroke of the pencil?

In happy hours, nature appears to us one with art; art perfected, — the work of genius. And the individual in whom simple tastes and susceptibility to all the great human influences overpowers the accidents of a local and special culture, is the best critic of art.

With a geometry of sunbeams the soul lays the foundations of nature.

In nature, all is useful, all is beautiful. It is therefore beautiful because it is alive, moving, reproductive; it is therefore useful because it is symmetrical and fair. Beauty will not come at the call of a legislature, nor will it repeat in England or America its history in Greece. It will come, as always, unannounced, and spring up between the feet of brave and earnest men.

Who loves nature? Who does not? Is it only poets, and men of leisure and cultivation, who live with her? No; but also hunters, farmers, grooms, and butchers, though they express their affection in their choice of life, and not in their choice of words.

All the facts of the animal economy, sex, nutriment, gestation, birth, growth, are symbols of the passage of the world into the soul of man, to suffer there a change, and reappear a new and higher fact. [The poet] uses forms according to the life, and not according to the form. This is true science. The poet alone knows astronomy, chemistry, vegetation, and animation, for he does not stop at these facts, but employs them as signs. He knows why the plain, or meadow of space, was strown with these flowers we call suns, and moons, and stars; why the great deep is adorned with animals, with men, and gods; for, in every word he speaks he rides on them as the horses of thought.

Nature, through all her kingdoms, insures herself. Nobody cares for planting the poor fungus; so she shakes down from the gills of one agaric countless spores, any one of which, being preserved, transmits new billions of spores to-morrow or [the] next day. The new agaric of this hour has a chance which the old one had not. This atom of seed is thrown into a new place, not subject to the accidents which destroyed its parent two rods off.

The sea, the mountain-ridge, Niagara, and every flower-bed, pre-exist, or super-exist, in precantations, which sail like odors in the air, and when any man goes by with an ear sufficiently fine, he overhears them, and endeavors to write them down as notes, without diluting or depraving them.

Nature does not like to be observed, and likes that we should be her fools and playmates. We may have the sphere for our cricket-ball, but not a berry for our philosophy. Direct strokes she never gave us power to make; all our blows glance, all our hits are accidents. Our relations to each other are oblique and casual.

The Laws of Nature

When, at night, I look at the moon and stars, I seem stationary, and they to hurry. Our love of the real draws us to permanence, but health of body consists in circulation, and sanity of mind in variety or facility of association. We need change of objects.

Life is not intellectual or critical, but sturdy. Its chief good is for well-mixed people who can enjoy what they find, without question. Nature hates peeping, and our mothers speak her very sense when they say, "Children, eat your victuals, and say no more of it."

Nature, as we know her, is no saint.

We fancy that we are strangers, and not so intimately domesticated in the planet as the wild man, and the wild beast and bird. But the exclusion reaches them also; reaches the climbing, flying, gliding, feathered and four-footed man. Fox and woodchuck, hawk and snipe, and bittern, when nearly seen, have no more root in the deep world than man, and are just such superficial tenants of the globe.

Nature and literature are subjective phenomena; every evil and every good thing is a shadow which we cast.

We may climb into the thin and cold realm of pure geometry and lifeless science, or sink into that of sensation. Between these extremes is the equator of life, of thought, of spirit, of poetry, — a narrow belt.

Nature never rhymes her children, nor makes two men alike.

Our action should rest mathematically on our substance. In nature, there are no false valuations. A pound of water in the ocean-tempest has no more gravity than in a midsummer pond. All things work exactly according to their quality, and according to their quantity; attempt nothing they cannot do, except man only. He has pretension; he wishes and attempts things beyond his force.

Life goes headlong. We chase some flying scheme, or we are hunted by some fear or command behind us. But if suddenly we encounter a friend we pause; our heat and hurry look foolish enough; now pause, now possession, is required, and the power to swell the moment from the resources of the heart. The moment is all, in all noble relations.

A man is but a little thing in the midst of the objects of nature, yet, by the moral quality radiating from his countenance, he may abolish all considerations of magnitude, and in his manners equal the majesty of the world.

Flowers and fruits are always fit presents; flowers, because they are a proud assertion that a ray of beauty outvalues all the utilities of the world.

At the gates of the forest, the surprised man of the world is forced to leave his city estimates of great and small, wise and foolish. The knapsack of custom falls off his back with the first step he makes into these precincts. Here is sanctity which shames our religions, and reality which discredits our heroes. Here we find nature to be the circumstance which dwarfs every other circumstance, and judges like a god all men that come to her.

The blue zenith is the point in which romance and reality meet. I think, if we should be rapt away into all that we dream of heaven, and should converse with Gabriel and Uriel, the upper sky would be all that would remain of our furniture.

The Laws of Nature

He who knows the most, he who knows what sweets and virtues are in the ground, the waters, the plants, the heavens, and how to come at these enchantments, is the rich and royal man. Only as far as the masters of the world have called in nature to their aid, can they reach the height of magnificence.

The sunset is unlike anything that is underneath it: it wants men. And the beauty of nature must always seem unreal and mocking, until the landscapes has human figures, that are as good as itself.

We see the foaming brook with compunction: if our own life flowed with the right energy, we would shame the brook.

Nature is always consistent, though she feigns to contravene her own laws. She keeps her laws, and seems to transcend them. She arms and equips an animal to find its place and living in the earth, and, at the same time, she arms and equips another animal to destroy it.

We talk of deviations from natural life, as if artificial life were not also natural. The smoothest curled courtier in the boudoirs of a palace has an animal nature, rude and aboriginal as a white bear, omnipotent to its own ends, and is directly related, there amid essences and billets-doux, to Himmaleh mountain-chains, and the axis of the globe.

A man does not tie his shoe without recognizing laws which bind the farthest regions of nature: moon, plant, gas, crystal, are concrete geometry and numbers.

It seems as if the day was not wholly profane, in which we have given heed to some natural object.

Exaggeration is in the course of things. Nature sends no creature, no man into the world, without adding a small excess of his proper quality.

The vegetable life does not content itself with casting from the flower or the tree a single seed, but it fills the air and earth with a prodigality of seeds, that, if thousands perish, thousands may plant themselves, that hundreds may come up, that tens may live to maturity, that, at least, one may replace the parent. All things betray the same calculated profusion.

But the craft with which the world is made, runs also into the mind and character of men. No man is quite sane; each has a vein of folly in his composition, a slight determination of blood to the head, to make sure of holding him hard to some one point which nature had taken to heart.

What splendid distance, what recesses of ineffable pomp and loveliness in the sunset! But who can go where they are, or lay his hand or plant his foot thereon?

The divine circulations never rest nor linger. Nature is the incarnation of a thought, and turns to a thought, again, as ice becomes water and gas. The world is mind precipitated, and the volatile essence is forever escaping again into the state of free thought.

Wild liberty develops an iron conscience. Want of liberty, by strengthening law and decorum, stupefies conscience.

We think our civilization near its meridian, but we are yet only at the cock-crowing and the morning star. In our barbarous society the influence of character is in its infancy.

One look at the face of heaven and earth lays all petulance at rest, and soothes us to wiser convictions. To the intelligent, nature converts itself into a vast promise, and will not be rashly explained. Her secret is untold.

We are amphibious creatures, weaponed for two elements, having two sets of faculties, the particular and the catholic. We adjust our instrument for general observation, and sweep the heavens as easily as we pick out a single figure in the terrestrial landscape.

Nature will not be Buddhist: she resents generalizing, and insults the philosopher in every moment with a million of fresh particulars.

We like to come to a height of land and see the landscape, just as we value a general remark in conversation. But it is not the intention of nature that we should live by general views.

If we cannot make voluntary and conscious steps in the admirable science of universals, let us see the parts wisely, and infer the genius of nature from the best particulars with a becoming charity.

Journals
1845–1873

Even though Emerson's worldview had crystallized by the mid-1840s, he was far from
putting his thoughts to rest. His journals show that he remained both physically and mentally
active well into old age. All the same, Emerson courted few new ideas in 1845 or beyond.
During the latter part of his life, he simply framed his beliefs better than he had before, adding
a little more shading to his observations of the world. No doubt personal losses — the death
of Margaret Fuller as well as the deaths of other friends and family members — darkened his
thoughts. Yet an abiding optimism, inspired by infinite nature, persists in his work.

◆ ◆ ◆

I go twice a week over Concord with Ellery, and, as we sit on the steep park at Conantum, we still have the same regret as oft before. Is all this beauty to perish? Shall none remake this sun and wind, the sky-blue river, the river-blue sky; the yellow meadow spotted with sacks and sheets of cranberry-pickers; the red bushes; the iron-gray house with just the color of the granite rock; the paths of the thicket, in which the only engineers are the cattle grazing on yonder hill; the wide, straggling wild orchard in which Nature has deposited every possible flavor in the apples of different trees?

Nature seems a dissipated hussy. She seduces us from all work.

How gladly, after three months sliding on snow, our feet find the ground again!

By atoms, by trifles, by sots, Heaven operates. The needles are nothing, the magnetism is all.

The Universe is like an infinite series of planes, each of which is a false bottom, and when we think our feet are planted now at last on the Adamant, the slide is drawn out from under us.

What is the oldest thing? A dimple or whirlpool in water. That is Genesis, Exodus, and all.

Who does not remember the south wind days when he was a boy, when his own hand had a strawberry scent?

I suppose you could never prove to the mind of the most ingenious mollusk that such a creature as a whale was possible.

Henry Thoreau is like the wood-god who solicits the wandering poet and draws him into antres vast and desarts idle,* and bereaves him of his memory, and leaves him naked, plaiting vines and with twigs in his hand.

Here I come down to the shore of the Sea and dip my hands in its miraculous waves. Here I am

I spoke of friendship but my friends and I are fishes in our habit. As for taking Thoreau's arm, I should as soon take the arm of an elm tree.

assured of the eternity, and can spare all omens, all prophecies, all religions, for I see and know that which they obscurely announce. I seem rich with earth and air and heaven; but the next morning I have lost my keys.

Another walk this Saturday afternoon with Ellery through the woods to the shore of Flint's Pond. The witch-hazel was in full bloom and from the highland we saw one of the best pictures of the New Hampshire Mountains. But Ellery said that when you come among them they are low, and nothing but cow pastures. I say, let us value the woods; they are full of solicitation. My wood lot has no price. I could not think of selling it for the money I gave for it. It is full of unknown and mysterious values.

Like the New England soil, my talent is good only whilst I work it. If I cease to task myself, I have no thoughts. This is a poor sterile Yankeeism. What I admire and love is the generous and spontaneous soil which flowers and fruits at all seasons.

---

* Taken from Shakespeare's *Othello*, "antres vast and desarts idle" refers to the distant and alien land where Othello was held captive.

The universe is only in transit, or, we behold it shooting the gulf from the past to the future.

Abuse is a pledge that you are felt. If they praise you, you will work no revolution.

We went to Willis's Pond in Sudbury and paddled across it, and took a swim in its water, coloured like sugar-baker's molasses. Nature, Ellery thought, is less interesting. Yesterday Thoreau told me it was more so, and persons less. I think it must always combine with man. Life is ecstatical, and we radiate joy and honour and gloom on the days and landscapes we converse with.

Old age. The world wears well. These autumn afternoons and well-marbled landscapes of green and gold and russet, and steel-blue river, and smoke-blue New Hampshire mountains, are and remain as bright and perfect pencilling as ever.

I think that a man should compare advantageously with a river, with an oak, with a mountain, endless flow, expansion, and grit.

Henry Thoreau rightly said, the other evening, talking of lightning-rods, that the only rod of safety was in the vertebrae of his own spine.

We cannot afford to live long, or Nature, which lives by illusions, will have disenchanted us too far for happiness.

The English believe that by mountains of fact they can climb into the heaven of thought and truth: so the builders of Babel believed.

Our fear of death is like our fear that summer will be short, but when we have had our swing of pleasure, our fill of fruit, and our swelter of heat, we say we have had our day.

I want a horse that will run all day like a wolf.

When I see the waves of Lake Michigan toss in the bleak snowstorm, I see how small and inadequate the common poet is.

Truth is always new and wild as the wild air, and is alive.

The most important effect of Copernicus was not on astronomy, but on Calvinism, — tapping the conceit of man; and geology introduces new measures of antiquity.

It must be admitted, that civilization is onerous and expensive; hideous expense to keep it up;– let it go, and be Indians again; but why Indians? – that is costly, too; the mud-turtle and trout life is easier and cheaper, and oyster, cheaper still.

How the landscape mocks the weakness of man! it is vast, beautiful, complete, and alive; and we can only dibble and step about, and dot it a little.

When a man says to me, "I have the intensest love of nature," at once I know that he has none.

To teach us the first lesson of humility, God set down man in these two vastitudes of Space and Time, yet is he such an incorrigible peacock that he thinks them only a perch to show his dirty feathers on.

Yesterday with Ellery at Flint's Pond. The pond was in its summer glory, the chestnuts in flower, two fishermen in a boat, thundertops in the sky, and the whole picture a study of all the secrets of landscape.

The great afternoon spends like fireworks, or festival of the gods, with a tranquil exultation, as of a boy that has launched his first boat, or his little balloon, and the experiment succeeds.

The woodchopper, by using the force of gravity, lets the planet chop his stick.

If a man is set on collecting diamonds, or Arabian horses, or an arboretum, or a particular piece of land, or a telescope, his heat makes the value.

The Laws of Nature

Henry [Thoreau] avoids commonplace, and talks birch bark to all comers, reduces them all to the same insignificance.

The most tender, the most radiant, the most sublime landscape is stark as tombstones, except seen by the thoughtful.

When I bought my farm, I did not know what a bargain I had in the bluebirds, bobolinks, and thrushes; as little did I know what sublime mornings and sunsets I was buying.

Thoreau. Perhaps his fancy for Walt Whitman grew out of his taste for wild nature, for an otter, a woodchuck, or a loon. He loved sufficiency, hated a sum that would not prove; loved Walt and hated Alcott.

The first care of a man settling in the country should be to open the face of the earth to himself by a little knowledge of Nature, or a great deal of knowledge, if he can, of birds, plants and astronomy; in short, the art of taking a walk.

People only see what they are prepared to see. Thus, who sees birds, except the hunter, or the ornithologist?

The spider finds it a good stand wherever he falls; he takes the first corner, and the flies make haste to come.

Williamstown. Of all tools, an observatory is the most sublime. And these mountains give an inestimable worth to Williamstown and Massachusetts. But, for the mountains, I don't quite like the proximity of a college and its noisy students. To enjoy the hills as [a] poet, I prefer simple farmers as neighbors.

The surprise and dazzle of beauty is such, that I thought to-day, that if beauty were the rule, instead of the exception, men would give up business.

I confess there is sometimes a caprice in fame, like the unnecessary eternity given to these minute shells and antediluvian fishes, leaves, ferns, yea, ripples and raindrops, which have come safe down through a vast antiquity, with all its shocks, upheavals, deluges, and volcanoes, wherein everything noble in art and humanity has perished, yet these snails, periwinkles, and worthless dead leaves come staring and perfect into our daylight. — What is fame, if every snail or ripple or raindrop shares it?

[Mount Mansfield, Vermont.] Perhaps it was a half-mile only from the [Mountain] House to the top of 'the Chin,' but it was a rough and grand walk. On such occasions, I always return to my fancy that the best use of wealth would be to carry a good professor of geology, and another of botany, with you.

The only place where I feel the joy of eminent domain is in my woodlot. My spirits rise whenever I enter it. I can spend the entire day there with hatchet or pruning-shears making paths, without a remorse of wasting time. I fancy the birds know me, and even the trees make little speeches or hint them.

The Laws of Nature

Nature is ever putting conundrums to us, and the savants, as in the girl's game of "Twenty Questions," are every month solving them successfully by skillful, exhaustive method. This success makes the student cheerful and confident, and his new illumination makes it impossible for him to acquiesce in the old barbarous routine, whether of politics, or religion, or commerce, or social arrangements. Nature will not longer be kinged, or churched, or colleged, or drawing-roomed as before.

God had infinite time to give us; but how did He give it? In one immense tract of a lazy millennium? No, but He cut it up into [a] neat succession of new mornings, and, with each, therefore, a new idea, new inventions, and new applications.

I do not know that I should feel threatened or insulted if a chemist should take his protoplasm or mix his hydrogen, oxygen, and carbon, and make an animalcule incontestably swimming and jumping before my eyes. I should only feel that it indicated that the day had arrived when the human race might be trusted with a new degree of power, and its immense responsibility; for these steps are not solitary or local, but only a hint of an advanced frontier supported by an advancing race behind it.

Naushon. I thought to-day, in these rare seaside woods, that if absolute leisure were offered me, I should run to the college or the scientific school which offered best lectures on Geology, Chemistry, Minerals, Botany, and seek to make the alphabets of those sciences clear to me. How could leisure or labour be better employed? 'Tis never late to learn them, and every secret opened goes to authorize our aesthetics.

Excerpts from
The Conduct of Life

The Conduct of Life, published in 1860, was the mature expression of Emerson's philosophy. Along with his journals from the same period, this book runs a little to the dark side. Here we find Emerson cultivating a coarse Darwinism while contemplating nature's ways. The Industrial Revolution was at full steam by this point in time, and the rate of scientific discovery was rapidly accelerating as a consequence. No doubt all this had a profound impact upon thinkers like Emerson who grounded their worldviews in physical realities. Suddenly, nature had more of an edge to it, and the role of humankind in the greater scheme of things seemed to be radically diminished. Despite all this, Emerson's deep respect for nature grew even deeper.

◆ ◆ ◆

The book of Nature is the book of Fate. She turns the gigantic pages, — leaf after leaf, — never re-turning one. One leaf she lays down, a floor of granite; then a thousand ages, and a bed of slate; a thousand ages, and a measure of coal; a thousand ages, and a layer of marl and mud: vegetable forms appear; her first misshapen animals, zoophyte, trilobium, fish; then, saurians, — rude forms, in which she has only blocked her future statue, concealing under these unwieldly monsters the fine type of her coming king. The face of the planet cools and dries, the races meliorate, and man is born. But when a race has lived its term, it comes no more again.

Nature is no sentimentalist, — does not cosset or pamper us. We must see that the world is rough and surly, and will not mind drowning a man or a woman; but swallows your ship like a grain of dust.

Famine, typhus, frost, war, suicide, and effete races, must be reckoned calculable parts of the system of the world. These are pebbles from the mountain, hints of the terms by which our life is walled up, and which show a kind of mechanical exactness, as of a loom or mill, in what we call casual or fortuitous events.

Whatever limits us, we call Fate. If we are brute and barbarous, the fate takes a brute and dreadful shape. As we refine, our checks become finer. If we rise to spiritual culture, the antagonism takes a spiritual form.

Rude and invincible except by themselves are the elements. So let man be. Let him empty his breast of his windy conceits, and show his lordship by manners and deeds on the scale of nature. Let him hold his purpose as with the tug of gravitation. No power, no persuasion, no bribe shall make him give up his point. A man ought to compare advantageously with a river, an oak, or a mountain. He shall have not less the flow, the expansion, and the resistance of these.

Thought dissolves the material universe, by carrying the mind up into a sphere where all is plastic.

The one serious and formidable thing in nature is a will.

But every jet of chaos which threatens to exterminate us, is convertible by intellect into wholesome force. Fate is unpenetrated causes. The water drowns ship and sailor, like a grain of dust. But learn to swim, trim your bark, and the wave which drowned it, will be cloven by it, and carry it, like its own foam, a plume and a power.

Eyes are found in light; ears in auricular air; feet on land; fins in water; wings in air; and, each creature where it was meant to be, with a mutual fitness. Every zone has its own *Fauna*. There is adjustment between the animal and its food, its parasite, its enemy. Balances are kept. It is not allowed to diminish in numbers, nor to exceed. The like adjustments exist for man.

Nature is no spendthrift, but takes the shortest way to her ends.

When there is something to be done, the world knows how to get it done. The vegetable eye makes leaf, pericarp, root, bark, or thorn, as the need is; the first cell converts itself into stomach, mouth, nose, or nail, according to the want: the world throws its life into a hero or a shepherd; and puts him where he is wanted.

Whilst the man is weak, the earth takes up him. He plants his brain and affections. By and by he will take up the earth, and have his gardens and vineyards in the beautiful order and productiveness of his thought. Every solid in the universe is ready to become fluid on the approach of the mind, and the power to flux it is the measure of the mind.

There is no need for foolish amateurs to fetch me to admire a garden of flowers, or a sun-gilt cloud, or a waterfall, when I cannot look with seeing splendor and grace. How idle to choose a random sparkle here or there, when the indwelling necessity plants the rose of beauty on the brow of chaos, and discloses the central intention of Nature to be harmony and joy.

All power is of one kind, a sharing of the nature of the world. The mind that is parallel with the laws of nature will be in the current of events, and strong with their strength.

Personal power, freedom, and the resources of nature strain every faculty of every citizen. We prosper with such vigor, that, like thrifty trees, which grow in spite of ice, lice, mice, and borers, so we do not suffer from the profligate swarms that fatten on the national treasury. The huge animals nourish huge parasites, and the rancor of the disease attests the strength of the constitution.

The longer the drought lasts, the more is the atmosphere surcharged with water. The faster the ball falls to the sun, the force to fly off is by so much augmented. And, in morals, wild liberty breeds iron conscience; natures with great impulses have great resources, and return from far.

All the elements whose aid man calls in, will sometimes become his masters, especially those of most subtle force. Shall he, then, renounce stream, fire, and electricity, or, shall he learn to deal with them?

I have never seen a man as rich as all men ought to be, or, with an adequate command of nature.

Nature has her own best mode of doing each thing, and she has somewhere told it plainly, if we will keep our eyes and ears open. If not, she will not be slow in undeceiving us, when we prefer our own way to hers.

The preservation of the species was a point of such necessity, that Nature has secured it at all hazards by immensely overloading the passion, at the risk of perpetual crime and disorder. So egotism has its root in the cardinal necessity by which each individual persists to be what he is.

Nature is reckless of the individual. When she has points to carry, she carries them. To wade in marshes and sea-margins is the destiny of certain birds, and they are so accurately made for this, that they are imprisoned in those places. Each animal out of its *habitat* would starve. To the physician, each man, each woman, is an amplification of one organ. A soldier, a locksmith, a bank-clerk, and a dancer could not exchange functions. And thus we are victims of adaptation.

A cheerful, intelligent face is the end of culture, and success enough. For it indicates the purpose of Nature and wisdom attained.

The fossil strata show us that Nature began with rudimental forms, and rose to the more complex, as fast as the earth was fit for their dwelling-place; and that the lower perish, as the higher appear. Very few of our race can be said to be yet finished men. We still carry sticking to us some remains of the preceding inferior quadruped organization.

Wise men read very sharply all your private history in your look and gait and behavior. The whole economy of nature is bent on expression. The tell-tale body is all tongues.

Men as naturally make a state, or a church, as caterpillars a web.

In our definitions, we grope after the *spiritual* by describing it as invisible. The true meaning of *spiritual* is *real*; that law which executes itself, which works without means, and which cannot be conceived as not existing. Men talk of "mere morality," — which is much as if one should say, 'poor God, with nobody to help him.' I find the omnipresence and the almightiness in the reaction of every atom in Nature. I can best indicate by examples those reactions by which every part of Nature replies to the purpose of the actor, — beneficently to the good, penally to the bad. Let us replace sentimentalism by realism, and dare to uncover those simple and terrible laws which, be they seen or unseen, pervade and govern.

'Tis a short sight to limit our faith in laws to those of gravity, of chemistry, of botany, and so forth. Those laws do not stop where our eyes lose them, but push the same geometry and chemistry up into the invisible plane of social and rational life, so that, look where we will, in a boy's game, or in the strifes of races, a perfect reaction, a perpetual judgement keeps watch and ward. And this appears in a class of facts which concerns all men, within and above their creeds.

If we meet no gods, it is because we harbor none. If there is grandeur in you, you will find grandeur in porters and sweeps. He only is rightly immortal, to whom all things are immortal.

Man is made of the same atoms as the world is, he shares the same impressions, predispositions, and destiny. When his mind is illuminated, when his heart is kind, he throws himself joyfully into the sublime order, and does, with knowledge, what the stones do by structure.

Nature makes fifty poor melons for one that is good, and shakes down a tree full of gnarled, wormy, unripe crabs, before you can find a dozen dessert apples; and she scatters nations of naked Indians, and nations of clothed Christians, with two or three good heads among them. Nature works very hard, and only hits the white once in a million throws.

Nature is a rag-merchant, who works up every shred and ort and end into new creations; like a good chemist, whom I found, the other day, in his laboratory, converting his old shirts into pure white sugar.

There is a tendency in things to right themselves, and the war or revolution or bankruptcy that shatters a rotten system, allows things to take a new and natural order. The sharpest evils are bent into that periodicity which makes the errors of planets, and the fevers and distempers of men, self-limiting. Nature is upheld by antagonism. Passions, resistance, danger, are educators. We acquire the strength we have overcome.

'Tis as easy to twist iron anchors, and braid cannons, as to braid straw, to boil granite as to boil water, if you take all the steps in order. Wherever there is failure, there is some giddiness, some superstition about luck, some step omitted, which Nature never pardons. The happy conditions of life may be had on the same terms.

What a parade we make of our science, and how far off, and at arm's length, it is from its objects! Our botany is all names, not powers: poets and romancers talk of herbs of grace and healing; but what does the botanist know of the virtues of his weeds?

All our science lacks a human side. The tenant is more than the house. Bugs and stamens and spores, on which we lavish so many years, are not finalities, and man, when his powers unfold in order, will take Nature along with him, and emit light into all her recesses. The human heart concerns us more than the poring into microscopes, and is larger than can be measured by the pompous figures of the astronomer.

If I could put my hand on the north star, would it be as beautiful? The sea is lovely, but when we bathe in it, the beauty forsakes all the near water. For the imagination and senses cannot be gratified at the same time.

Beauty is the form under which the intellect prefers to study the world.

Elegance of form in bird or beast, or in the human figure, marks some excellence of structure: or beauty is only an invitation from what belongs to us. 'Tis a law of botany, that in plants, the same virtues follow the same forms. It is a rule of largest application, true in a plant, true in a loaf of bread, that in the construction of any fabric or organism, any real increase of fitness to its end, is an increase of beauty.

Beauty rests on necessities. The line of beauty is the result of perfect economy. The cell of the bee is built at that angle which gives the most strength with the least wax; the bone or the quill of the bird gives the most alar strength, with the least weight.

All the facts in Nature are nouns of the intellect, and make the grammar of the eternal language. Every word has a double, treble, or centuple use and meaning. What! has my stove and pepper-pot a false bottom! I cry you mercy, good shoe-box! I did not know you were a jewel-case. Chaff and dust begin to sparkle, and are clothed about with immortality. And there is a joy in perceiving the representative or symbolic character of a fact, which no bare fact or event can ever give. There are no days in life so memorable as those which vibrated to some stroke of the imagination.

Into every beautiful object, there enters somewhat immeasurable and divine, and just as much into form bounded by outlines, like mountains on the horizon, as into tones of music, or depths of space. Polarized light showed the secret architecture of bodies; and when the *second-sight* of the mind is opened, now one color or form or gesture, and now another, has a pungency, as if a more interior ray had been emitted, disclosing its deep holdings in the frame of things.

Health and appetite impart the sweetness to sugar, bread, and meat. We fancy that our civilization has got on far, but we still come back to our primers.

The intellect sees that every atom carries the whole of Nature; that the mind opens to omnipotence; that, in the endless striving and ascents, the metamorphosis is entire, so that the soul doth not know itself in its own act, when that act is perfected. There is illusion that shall deceive even the elect. There is illusion that shall deceive even the performer of the miracle.

Is not our faith in the impenetrability of matter more sedative than narcotics? You play with jackstraws, balls, bowls, horse and gun, estates and politics; but there are finer games before you. Is not time a pretty toy? Life will show you masks that are worth all your carnivals. Yonder mountain must migrate into your mind. The fine star-dust and nebulous blur in Orion, "the portentous year

Our conversation with Nature is not just what it seems. The cloud-rack, the sunrise and sunset glories, rainbows, and northern lights are not quite so spheral as our childhood thought them; and the part our organization plays in them is too large.

of Mizar and Alcor," must come down and be dealt with in your household thought. What if you shall come to discern that the play and playground of all this pompous history are radiations from yourself, and that the sun borrows his beams? What terrible questions we are learning to ask!

One would think from the talk of men, that riches and poverty were a great matter; and our civilization mainly respects it. But the Indians say, that they do not think the white man with his brow of care, always toiling, afraid of heat and cold, and keeping within doors, has any advantage of them. The permanent interest of every man is, never to be in a false position, but to have the weight of Nature to back him in all that he does. Riches and poverty are a thick or thin costume; and our life — the life of all of us — identical. For we transcend the circumstance continually, and taste the real quality of existence; as in our employments, which only differ in the manipulations, but express the same laws; or in our thoughts, which wear no silks, and taste no ice-creams. We see God face to face every hour, and know the savor of Nature.

We cannot write the order of the variable winds. How can we penetrate the law of our shifting moods and susceptibility? Yet they differ as all and nothing. Instead of the firmament of yesterday, which our eyes require, it is to-day an eggshell which coops us in; we cannot even see what or where our stars of destiny are.

Selected Bibliography

Bode, Carl, ed. *Ralph Waldo Emerson: A Profile*. New York: Hill and Wang, 1969.

Brooks, Van Wyck. *The Flowering of New England, 1815–1865*. New York: Dutton, 1937.

Emerson, Ralph Waldo. *The Conduct of Life*. Garden City, NY: Doubleday, n.d.

———. *Emerson's Essays*, edited by Irwin Edman. New York: Thomas Y. Crowell Company, 1961.

———. *The Heart of Emerson's Journals*, edited by Bliss Perry. Boston: Houghton Mifflin, 1926.

———. *The Journals of Ralph Waldo Emerson*, edited by Robert N. Linscott. New York: Random House, 1960.

———. *Nature: A Facsimile of the First Edition*, edited by Jaroslav Pelikan. Boston: Beacon Press, 1989.

———. *The Works of Ralph Waldo Emerson*. Roslyn, NY: Black's Readers Service, n.d.

Nash, Roderick. *Wilderness and the American Mind*. New Haven, CT: Yale University, 1982.

Porte, Joel, and Saundra Morris, eds. *The Cambridge Companion to Ralph Waldo Emerson*. Cambridge, England; New York: Cambridge University Press, 1999.

Richardson Jr., Robert D. *Emerson: The Mind on Fire*. Berkeley: University of California Press, 1995.

List of Watercolor Illustrations in this Edition

All the watercolors in this book are by Roderick MacIver, founder of *Heron Dance*.

Select watercolors from this list are available as full-color, limited-edition prints on the *Heron Dance* website (www.herondance.org) by typing the title in the search bar. If you have trouble finding the image you would like or do not have access to the internet, please call *Heron Dance* toll free at 888-304-3766 or send an email to heron@herondance.org.

About the Author

Ralph Waldo Emerson (1803–1882) was one of the most thought-provoking writers of the 19th century, influencing Henry David Thoreau, Walt Whitman, and many others, both at home and abroad. He was also among the first to incorporate the power of wild nature into his worldview, thus giving birth to Transcendentalism—a distinctly American philosophy. Here we offer excerpts from his writings, gleaned from personal journals as well as published works, to provide a glimpse into the mind of a true lover of nature.

About the Editor

Walt McLaughlin is an avid outdoorsman who has written extensively about his wilderness experiences. He received a degree in philosophy from Ohio University in 1977 and has been studying the works of Thoreau, Emerson, and other nature writers ever since. His poetry and prose have appeared in *Adirondac, Northeast, Vermont Life, Writing Nature*, and many other periodicals. He has several books in print, including a collection of short narratives, *Backcountry Excursions* (Wood Thrush Books, 2005), and a slender volume of poems, *A Hungry Happiness* (Timberline Press, 2006). His narrative about hiking Vermont's Long Trail end-to-end, *Forest Under My Fingernails*, has been reprinted recently by Heron Dance Press. He lives in St. Albans, Vermont, with his wife Judy.

Heron Dance

Heron Dance Press & Art Studio is a nonprofit 501(c)(3) organization founded in 1995 by artist Roderick MacIver and run today with editor and writer Ann O'Shaughnessy. It is a work of love, an effort to produce something that is thought-provoking and beautiful. Through our website, quarterly journal, workshops, free weekly e-newsletter and watercolors, *Heron Dance* celebrates the seeker's journey and the beauty and mystery of the natural world.

We invite you to visit us at www.herondance.org to view the many beautiful watercolors by Roderick MacIver and to browse the hundreds of pages of book excerpts, poetry, essays, and interviews of authors and artists. In our studio store, we offer *Heron Dance* notecards, limited-edition prints, and original paintings, as well as dozens of hard-to-find books, music, and films.

To receive our free weekly email — *A Pause for Beauty* — which features a new watercolor and a poem or excerpt, just click on the *Pause for Beauty* link found on our website or contact us at the number below.

ALSO FROM HERON DANCE PRESS
All titles feature Roderick MacIver watercolors

A Death on the Barrens

Five young men canoe through Canada's arctic and must find their way home, after the death of their leader, Art Moffatt, from hypothermia. Winter closes in, the group runs out of food. This book is both George Grinnell's account of a journey through then un-mapped northern lakes and rivers, and a story of the spiritual awakening of the young men on the trip. *A Death on the Barrens* was first published in 1996, and quickly sold out. This second edition contains watercolors by Roderick MacIver. 192 pages.

#6084   A Death on the Barrens — $19.95

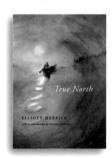

True North
with an introduction by Lawrence Millman

In 1929, at the age of 24, Elliott Merrick left his position as an advertising executive in New Jersey and headed up to Labrador to work as an unpaid volunteer for the Grenfell Mission. In 1933 he wrote True North about his experiences in the northern wilderness, living and working with trappers, Indians and with the nurse he met and married in a remote community. The book describes the hard work and severe conditions, along with the joy and friendship he and his wife experienced. 320 pages

#6086   True North — $19.95

Sleeping Island
A Journey to the Edge of the Barrens

In *Sleeping Island*, Prentice G. Downes records a journey made in 1939 of a North that was soon to be no more, a landscape and a people barely touched by the white man. His respect for the Native Indians and the Inuit, their ways of life, and his love of their land shine through this richly descriptive work. With the kind permission of the Downes family, *Heron Dance* has republished this book. 288 pages.

#6083   Sleeping Island — $19.95

Forest Under My Fingernails
Reflections and Encounters on Vermont's Long Trail

Years ago we excerpted this book about Walt McLaughlin's wilderness trek. The book sold out but recently has been reprinted. His reflections and encounters are beautifully told. We highly recommend it. 192 pages.

#6085   *Forest Under My Fingernails* — $15.95

Heron Dance Book of Love and Gratitude

Heron Dance celebrates the open heart and the beauty and mystery that surround us with this book of poetry, book, and interview excerpts. Designed by Ann O'Shaughnessy, it contains forty-eight watercolors by Roderick MacIver and selections from the written works of Helen Keller, Dostoevsky, and Henry Miller, among many others. 80 pages.

#1602   *Heron Dance Book of Love and Gratitude* — $12.00

This Ecstasy

This courageous and beautiful book of poems by John Squadra explores, with simplicity, the truths of love and a spiritual life. Some poems are very erotic. Some poems expose the truths of life we all share.

#6087   *This Ecstasy* — $10.95

A Natural Wisdom
Gleanings from the Journals of Henry David Thoreau

Walt McLaughlin selects 80 entries from Thoreau's journals that are thought-provoking and insightful. 62 pages.

#6019   *A Natural Wisdom* — $10.00

Earth, My Likeness
Nature Poetry of Walt Whitman

A carefully selected collection of poems alongside Roderick MacIver's watercolor art creates a grand tribute. Edited by Howard Nelson. 144 pages.

#6088   *Earth, My Likeness* — $11.95